THE NATURE NOTEBOOK SERIES

EDITED BY

ANNA BOTSFORD COMSTOCK

THE COMMON ANIMAL NOTEBOOK

BY

ANNA BOTSFORD COMSTOCK

THE COMSTOCK PUBLISHING COMPANY

ITHACA, NEW YORK

This Edition

Published 2020

By HearthRoom Press

Illustrations by: Louis Agassiz Fuertes

Original Work

By

The Comstock Publishing Company

PREFACE

This little Notebook of Common Animals is primarily a supplement to the animal studies in the Handbook of Nature Study. It's plan is to give to the pupil those questions about the life of each animal that will lead him to a knowledge of its habits. A story written by the pupil which includes answers to as many questions as possible will form the text, and the outlines, colored by the pupil, will form the illustrations of the book. Whenever it is possible the outlines should be colored from life; in the case of the domestic animals this is easily accomplished and it is also possible in the case of most common wild animals, like the squirrel and the rabbit. However, it may not be practicable for the pupils to paint the pictures from nature, and in that case, they may be copied from the animal books, illustrated in color. The best book for this purpose, known to the author, is "Wild Animals of North America," published by the National Geographic Society in Washington. However, there are other books like Reed's Animal Guide, which may be used. A very good plan would be to have some pupil, skilled in water-color, paint a set of the loose-leaf outlines which could be mounted on cardboard and hang on the wall of the schoolroom and used as a model for the younger pupils to copy.

The Questions about the animals are answered in the Teacher's Story in the Handbook of Nature Study, except in the case of a few animals which were added to make a number more complete; for these, special references are given. Mention is also made of good descriptive stories to be used in supplementary reading.

The pupil should be inspired to desire to complete his own notebook so that he can have an animal book of his own writing and illustrating.

Supplementary Reading

The Handbook of Nature Study gives quite complete accounts of the following animals: bat, cat, chipmunk, cow, dog, fox, goat, horse, mouse, muskrat, newt, pig, rabbit, raccoon, sheep, skunk, snake, squirrel, toad, turtle, and woodchuck.

The Pet Book (Comstock) discusses the habits and care of the following animals: all those mentioned above except the muskrat and in addition the donkey, guinea pig, opossum, ferret, porcupine, prairie dog, flying squirrel.

The above books give at the end of each chapter, references to interesting stories and accounts of these animals.

For interesting descriptions of a gopher and the mole see American Animals by Stone and Cram.

INDEX

Questions to be answered and points to be covered in writing the story of

THE CHIPMUNK

1. Do you see the chipmunk climbing around the trees like the red squirrel? How high in a tree have you ever seen a chipmunk?

2. What are the chipmunk's colors above and below? How many stripes has it? Where are they and what are their colors? Do you think that these stripes conceal the animal when among the grasses and bushes? How?

3. Compare the tails of the chipmunk and the red squirrel. Which is longer and bushier? Tell if you can, the special advantages to the chipmunk in having this less bushy tail.

4. What does the chipmunk eat? How does it carry its food? How does it differ in this respect to the red squirrel? Does it store its food for winter use? How does it prepare its nuts? How does it hold its food while eating?

5. Where does the chipmunk make its home? How does it carry away soil from its burrow? How many entrances are there? How is the den arranged inside? Does it live in the same den the year round? When does it retire to its den in the fall? When does it come out in the spring?

6. Does the chipmunk do any damage to crops? What seeds does it distribute? At what time do the little chipmunks appear in the spring?

7. Observe carefully the different tones of the chipmunk and compare its chattering with that of the squirrel.

Color: The head of the chipmunk is brown with cheek-pockets yellowish; the back is gray the hind legs and thighs reddish brown; there is a narrow black stripe along the middle of the back; each side has two black stripes with a buff stripe between them; the sides of the body are buff, the lower side is white; the tail is grayish above and reddish brown below.

The Chipmunk

THE STORY OF THE CHIPMUNK

Questions to be answered and points to be covered in writing the story of

THE RED SQUIRREL OR CHICKAREE

1. Where have you seen a red squirrel? Does the squirrel trot along or leap when running on the ground? Does it run straight ahead or stop at intervals for observation? How does it act when looking to see if the 'coast is clear?'

2. When climbing a tree, does it go straight up, or move around the trunk? How does it hide itself behind a tree trunk and observe the passer-by? Does it go down the tree head first? Is it able to climb out on the small branches? Of what advantage is this to it?

3. How does it pass from tree to tree? How does it act when preparing to jump? How does it hold its legs and tail when in the air during a jump from branch to branch?

4. How are the squirrel's eyes placed? Do you think it can see behind as well as in front all the time?

5. Are its legs long or short? Are its hind legs stronger and longer than the front legs? Why? Do its paws have claws? How does it use its paws when eating and in making its toilet?

6. Describe the squirrel's tail. Is it as long as the body? Of what use is it in the winter?

7. What is the food of the squirrel during the autumn? Winter? Spring? Summer? Where does it store food for the winter? How does it carry nuts? Has it cheek-pouches like the chipmunk for carrying food? Does it stay in its nest all winter living on stored food like the chipmunk? Describe its teeth.

8. Where does the red squirrel make its winter home? Does it also have a summer home, if so, of what is it made and where built? In what sort of nest are the young born and reared? At what time of the year are the young born?

9. How much of the squirrel language can you understand? How does it express surprise, excitement, anger, or joy during the nut harvest? Describe or sketch the tracks made by the squirrel in the snow.

Color: The red squirrel is reddish brown on its back and upper side of the tail; the sides are gray; the lower side of the body is white with a narrow black stripe along the side where the white and gray join.

The Red Squirrel

THE STORY OF THE RED SQUIRREL

Questions to be answered and points to be covered in writing the story of

THE COTTON-TAIL RABBIT

1. What are the two most noticeable peculiarities of the rabbit? Of what use are such large ears? How are the ears held when the rabbit is resting? When startled? When not quite certain about the direction of the noise? When the rabbit wishes to make an observation to see if there is danger coming, how does it hold its ears? How are the ears held when running?

2. Do you think the rabbit has a keen sense of smell? Describe the movements of the nostrils and explain the reason. How does it move its head to be sure of getting the scent?

3. What peculiarity is there in the upper lip? How would this be an aid to the rabbit when gnawing? Describe the teeth; how do these differ from those of the mouse or squirrel? How does it eat a stem of grass? Note the rabbit's whiskers. How are the eyes placed so that the rabbit can see forward and backward?

4. Why is it advantageous to the rabbit to have such long, strong, hind legs? Compare them in size with the front legs. Compare the front and hind feet. How many toes on each? How are the bottoms of the feet protected? Are the front feet ever used for holding food like the squirrels? In what position are the front legs when the rabbit is resting? When it is standing? When lifted up for observation?

5. What sort of tracks does the cotton-tail make in the snow? Sketch them. How would you know which way the rabbit was going? When were these tracks made, by night or by day? What does the rabbit do during the day?

6. How does the cotton-tail escape being seen? Describe its coat. Of what use is the white fluff beneath the tail?

7. In making its toilet how does the rabbit clean its face, ears, feet, and fur?

8. What do the cotton-tails feed upon during the summer? During the winter? Do they ever do much damage?

9. Describe the cotton-tail's nest. What is it called? Describe the nest made for the young by the mother. Of what is the bed composed? Of what is the coverlet made and for what used?

10. 10. What are the cotton-tail's enemies? How does it escape them? Do you think that a dog or a fox could follow it in a briar patch? Do rabbits ever fight their enemies? If so, how? How do they show anger? Do they stamp with the front or the hind foot?

Color: The cotton-tail rabbit is gray along the back and hind quarters; the sides and head are brown; the body is white below with a gray band across the breast; the tail is white on the underside which is the part showing in this outline.

The Cotton-tail Rabbit

THE STORY OF THE COTTON-TAIL RABBIT

Questions to be answered and points to be covered in writing the story of

THE TURTLE

1. How much can you see of the turtle when it is walking? If you disturb it what does it do? How much of it can you see then? Can you see more of it from the lower side than the upper? What is the advantage to the turtle of having such a shell?

2. Compare the upper shell with the lower as follows: How are they shaped differently? What is their difference in color? Would it be a disadvantage to the turtle if the upper shell were as light colored as the lower? Why? Where are the two grown together?

3. Is the border of the upper shell different from the central portion in color and markings? Is the edge smooth or scalloped?

4. How far does the turtles head project from the front of the shell? What is the shape of the head? With what colors and pattern is it marked? Describe the eyes. How are they protected? How does the turtle wink? Can you discover the little eyelid which comes up from below to cover the eye? Describe the nose and nostrils.

5. Describe the mouth. Are there any teeth? With what does it bite off its food? Describe the movement of the throat. Why is this?

6. What is the shape of the leg? How is it marked? How many claws on the front feet? Are any of the toes webbed? On which feet are the webbed toes? Why should they be webbed? Describe the way a turtle swims. Which feet are used for oars?

7. Describe the tail. How much can be seen from above when the turtle is walking? What becomes of it, when the turtle is frightened?

8. How much of the turtle's body can you see? What is its color? Is it rough or smooth?

9. What are the turtle's enemies? How does it escape from them? What noise does the turtle make when frightened?

10. Do all turtles live for part of the time in water? What is their food and where do they find it? Write an account of all the species of turtles that you know.

11. How do turtle eggs look? Where are they laid? How are they hidden?

Color: The turtle should be colored according to the specimen under observation; each species has its own colors and markings.

The Turtle

THE STORY OF THE TURTLE

Questions to be answered and points to be covered in writing the story of

THE STRIPED GOPHER

1. Where do you see the striped gopher? How does it look when it stands up on its hind feet? Why does it stand this way?

2. Describe the stripes on the gopher's back. What color is it underneath? What color beneath the chin? How do the gophers colors and stripes protect it from being seen by its enemies?

3. Where does the gopher make its home? Where is the home of the little gophers and how is it made comfortable? How does the gopher dig its burrow? How does it carry out the dirt?

4. Upon what does the gopher feed? Where does it find its food?

5. What are its enemies and how does it escape them?

6. Describe the eyes. Do you think it can see well?

7. How do the ears look?

8. Describe the tail and its color.

9. Where does the gopher spend the winter? What does it store for winter food? Where does it store the food?

10. Do you think the striped gopher benefits or damages the farm?

Color: The gopher's back is striped with six buff bands and seven broader brown bands which are spotted with white; the lower side of the body is dull buff. Buff is pale brownish yellow.

The Striped Gopher

THE STORY OF THE STRIPED GOPHER

Questions to be answered and points to be covered in writing the story of

THE OPOSSUM

1. How large is the opossum? What color is the fur? Describe its fur.

2. Describe the eyes, the ears and mouth. Has it "whiskers" like that of a cat?

3. Do the opossums' feet look like little hands? Are they used like hands for grasping?

4. Describe the tail, it's length and its covering. For what is it used?

5. Where does the opossum make its nest? Does it sleep in this nest all winter?

6. Where does the mother opossum carry her little ones? What animal which we see in the zoo carries its little ones in a similar way?

7. When the little ones are large enough to come out of the pocket how do they keep from falling off their mother's back when playing? When frightened, what do they do?

8. What does the opossum feed upon? Does it do its hunting during the day or the night? What does it do daytimes?

9. Where did we get the saying, "playing possum?" Why does the opossum do this queer thing? Do you know of other animals that feign death when attacked?

10. 10. Why is the opossum hunted?

Color: The general color of the opossum is grayish white; the legs are brownish black, the feet black and the toes white; the ears are black with white tips; the tail is black at base and flash color toward the tip; the head throat and underparts are white. Tips of ears, nose and toes pinkish.

The Opossum

THE STORY OF THE OPOSSUM

Questions to be answered and points to be covered in writing the story of

THE FLYING SQUIRREL

1. How does the flying squirrel differ from other squirrels? Why is it called "flying squirrel?" How does it fly? What does it have instead of wings?

2. Of what advantage is it to the squirrel to be able to jump from a tree-top without danger of falling?

3. What is the color of the flying squirrel above and below? What sort of fur has it?

4. Describe the eyes of the squirrel. How do they differ from the eyes of the red squirrel?

5. Why do we seldom see this squirrel in the day time? When is it most active?

6. Where is its nest? Where does it stay during the winter/ Do several live together? Does it make a summer nest as well?

7. What is its food and how does it get it? Does it store food for use in winter?

8. When are the young ones to be found?

9. Tell about some pet flying squirrel of which you know about or about which you have read.

10. How can you find flying squirrels out in the woods?

Color: The flying squirrel is dull brown tinged with reddish above and white underneath; it is whiteish on the sides of the neck and below the ears.

The Flying Squirrel

THE STORY OF THE FLYING SQUIRREL

Questions to be answered and points to be covered in writing the story of

THE DONKEY

1. Compare the donkey with the horse in the following characteristics: Is its head wider than that of the horse? Is its neck shorter? Are its ears longer? Is the hoof narrower, longer and more upright? Is its coat more shaggy? How is the tail shaped differently?

2. Of what use would such large ears be to the donkey if it were a wild animal? The donkeys are still wild animals in Persia and roam about in herds, where they are hunted for their flesh and their hides.

3. What advantage is it to the donkey in climbing mountain trails to have such a thick hoof?

4. What is the color of the donkey and what are the markings on its coat?

5. Why does the donkey bray? Do you think it is for the same reason that a horse whinnies?

6. Is the donkey as expensive to keep as a horse? Will it thrive on food too poor to satisfy a horse?

7. What means of fighting has the donkey? How does it manage to kick, hitting just the place it wishes to?

8. Where is the donkey much used in the United States? In Europe? How does it usually carry its load?

9. Who first introduced donkeys into the United States?

10. What sort of treatment has developed obstinacy in the donkey?

Color: Mouse gray with a dark line along the backbone and a dark transverse line across the shoulders.

The Donkey

THE STORY OF THE DONKEY

Questions to be answered and points to be covered in writing the story of

THE COMMON MOLE

1. What do you notice first when you look at a mole? How do the front feet differ from the hind feet?

2. What does the mole use its large front feet for? How do the strong claws help?

3. Where does the mole live? Does it have a nest in the earth? Why does it make long galleries underground?

4. In digging the galleries, how does it use its pointed nose; its front feet and its hind feed?

5. What evidence do we see on the ground when a mole is burrowing underneath? Do we like this?

6. What does the mole feed upon? Is this a benefit to us?

7. How does the moles snout differ from that of a mouse? How does this long pointed snout aid the mole in digging?

8. Describe the mole's eyes. Does it need eyes when it lives always below the surface of the earth?

9. Can you find that the mole has any ears? Does it need any ears? What would happen to its ears if they were like those of the mouse?

10. 10. Describe the mole's fur. Why is this kind of fur very useful to it? Does it lie smoothly in any direction?

11. 11. Is the moles tail long or short? If it were as long as that of the house-mouse would it be in the way?

12. Where does the mole live in winter?

Color: The fur of the mole is silvery gray shaded with slate gray; the feet and tip of the snout are pinkish.

The Mole

THE STORY OF THE COMMON MOLE

Questions to be answered and points to be covered in writing the story of

THE MUSKRAT

1. How long is the largest muskrat you ever saw? How much of the whole length is the tail? Is the general shape of the body short and heavy or long and slender? Why is this animal called muskrat?

2. Describe the muskrats eyes, ears and teeth. For what are the teeth especially fitted? Has the muskrat any whiskers?

3. Compare the front and hind legs as to size and shape? Is there a web between the toes of the hind feet? What does this indicate? Do you think that the muskrat is a good swimmer?

4. Describe the muskrat fur. Compare the outer and under coat. The color of the muskrat above and below? Under what name is muskrat fur sold?

5. Describe the tail. What is its covering? How is it flattened? What do you think this strong, flattened tail is used for?

6. How is the muskrat fitted to live in the water in the following particulars: Feet? Tail? Fur?

7. How much of the muskrat can you see when it is swimming? How long can it stay under water when diving?

8. What is the food of the muskrat? Where does it find it? How does it prepare the food for eating? Does it seek its food during the day or night?

9. Describe the structure of the muskrat's winter lodge, or cabin in the following particulars: It's size? Where built? Of what material? How many rooms in it? Are these rooms above or below the water level? Of what is the bed made? How is the nest ventilated? How is it arranged so that the entrance is not closed by the ice? Is such a home built by one or more muskrats? How many live within it?

10. Describe the muskrat's burrow in the bank in the following particulars: Is the entrance above or below water? Where and how is the nest made? Is it ventilated? Does it have a back door leading out upon the land?

11. What are the muskrat's enemies? How does it escape them? How does it fight? Is it a courageous animal? How does the muskrat give warning to its fellows when it perceives danger? At what time of year is it comparatively safe? At what time is it exposed to the greatest danger? Compare the habits of the muskrat with those of the beaver.

Color: The muskrat is dark brown above with dull yellow shading on the sides; the underparts, the throat and the lips are grayish white; there is a brown spot on the chin.

The Muskrat

THE STORY OF THE MUSKRAT

Questions to be answered and points to be covered in writing the story of

THE WOODCHUCK OR GROUND-HOG

1. Where is the woodchuck found? On what does it live? At what time of day does it feed? How does it act when startled?

2. Is the woodchuck a good fighter? With what weapons does it fight? What are its enemies? How does it escape its enemies when in or out of its burrow? How does it look when running?

3. What noises does the woodchuck make and what do they mean?

4. How does the woodchuck make its burrow? Where is it likely to be situated? Where is the earth placed which is taken from the burrow? How does the woodchuck bring it out? How is the burrow made so that the woodchuck is not drowned in the case of heavy rains? In what direction do the underground galleries go? Where is the nest placed in relation to the galleries? Of what is the nest made? How is the bedding carried in? Of what special use is the nest?

5. Are there paths leading to the entrance of the burrow? How does the woodchuck look to see if enemies are coming?

6. How many woodchucks inhabit the same burrow? Are there likely to be one or more back doors to the burrow? What for? How do the back doors differ from the front?

7. What is the woodchuck's color? Is its fur long or short? Coarse or fine? Thick or sparse? Is the skin thick or thin?

8. Compare the front and hind feet and describe the differences in their size and shape. Are either or both slightly webbed? Explain how both front and hind feet and legs are adapted by their shape to help the woodchuck. Is the tail long or short? How does it assist the animal in sitting up?

9. What is the shape of the woodchuck's ear? Can it hear well? Why are the ears not filled with soil when the animal is burrowing? Of what use are the long front teeth, the incisors? Describe the eyes.

10. How does the woodchuck prepare for winter? Where and how does it pass the winter? Did you ever know a woodchuck to come out on Candlemas Day* to look for its shadow?

11. When does the woodchuck appear in the spring? Compare its general appearance in the fall and in the spring and explain.

12. When are the young woodchucks born? How does the mother woodchuck care for her young?

Color: The woodchuck is yellowish gray shaded with blackish and reddish brown; the underparts are reddish brown; the feet are black.

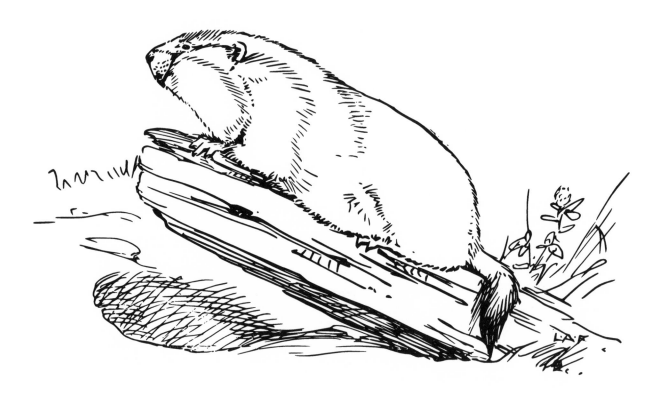

The Woodchuck

THE STORY OF THE WOODCHUCK

Questions to be answered and points to be covered in writing the story of

THE BAT

1. At what time of day do we see bats flying? Describe how the bat's flight differs from that of birds. Why do bats dart about so rapidly?

2. Look at a captive bat and describe its wings. Can you see what makes the framework of the wings? Do you see the three finger bones extending out into the wings? How do the hind legs support the wing? The tail? Is the wing membrane covered with fur? Is it thick and leathery or thin and silky and elastic? How does the bat fold up its wings?

3. In what position does the bat rest? Does it ever hang by its thumb-hooks?

4. Can you see whether the knees of the hind legs bend upward or downward? How does the bat act when trying to walk or crawl? How does it use its thumb-hooks in doing this?

5. What does the bat do daytimes? Where does it stay during the day? Do many bats congregate together in their roosts?

6. Describe the bats head, including the ears, eyes, nose and mouth. What is the general expression? Do you think it can see and hear well? How is its mouth fitted for catching insects? Does it shut its mouth while chewing or keep it open? Do you think that bats can see by daylight?

7. What noises does a bat make? How does it act when you try to touch it? Can it bite severely?

8. Do you know how the mother bat cares for her young? How does she carry them? At What time of year may we expect to find them?

9. When making its toilet, how does a bat clean its wings? Its face? Its back? Its feet? Do you know if it is very clean in its habits?

10. How and where do the bats pass the winter? How are they beneficial to us? Are they ever harmful?

Color: The bat is glossy brown above, yellowish below and the wing membranes are grayish brown.

The Bat

THE STORY OF THE BAT

Questions to be answered and points to be covered in writing the story of

THE SKUNK

1. How large is a skunk? Describe its fur. Where does the black and white occur in the fur? Of what use is the white to the skunk? Is the fur valuable? What is its commercial name?

2. What is the shape of the skunks head? The general shape of the body? The tail? Are the front legs longer or shorter than the hind legs? Describe the front feet. For what are they used?

3. Where and how does the skunk make its nest? Does it sleep like a woodchuck during the winter? What is its food? How does it catch its prey? Does it hunt for its food during the day or night? Does the skunk ever hurry? Is it afraid? How does it protect itself from its enemies? Do you think that the skunks freedom from fear has rendered the animal less intelligent?

4. At what time do the skunk kittens appear? Have you ever seen little skunks playing? If so, describe their antics. How is the nest made soft for the young ones?

5. How does the skunk benefit from farmers? Does it ever do them any injury? Do you think that it does more good than harm?

6. Describe the skunks tracks as follows: How many toes show in the track? Does the palm or heal show? Are the tracks near together? Do they form a single or a double line?

Color: The skunk is black with a white patch on the neck of the neck back of the head from which two white stripes extend down the back and along each side of the tail; there is a white stripe in the face.

The Skunk

THE STORY OF THE SKUNK

Questions to be answered and points to be covered in writing the story of

THE RACCOON

1. What kind of fur has the raccoon? Why does it need such a heavy covering? Describe the color of the fur. Describe the tail. Of what use is such a large and bushy tail to the animal?

2. Describe the raccoon's face. How is it marked? What is its expression? Describe the eyes and the ears; the nose. Has it teeth resembling those of the cat and dog?

3. Describe the raccoon's feet. How many toes on the front feet? How many on the hind feet? How does this differ from the cat and dog? How do the front and hind feet differ in appearance? Can both be used as hands?

4. Why do raccoon's like to live near the water? What do they find of interest there? How do they prepare their meat before eating it? How does the raccoon handle its meat while eating it?

5. What do raccoon's eat and how do they get their food? Which of our crops are they likely to damage? What other damage do they do? Have you ever heard raccoon's cry or whistle during August nights in the cornfields?

6. Where have you found raccoon tracks? How do they differ from those of the fox or dog? How far are the footprints apart? Can you see the heel and toe prints? Do you see the tracks of all four feet? Are the tracks in a straight line like those of the cat? What is the size of the track, the length, the breadth?

7. How do raccoon's arrange themselves for a nap in a tree? How do they cover the head? How is the tail used? Do you think this bushy tail would help to keep the animal warm in winter? Do raccoon's sleep most during the day or night?

8. At what time of year are raccoon's fattest? Leanest? Why? Do they ever come out of their nests in winter? Do they live together or singly in winter?

9. At what time of year are the young raccoon's born? Do you know how they look when they are young? How are they cared for by their parents?

10. Are the raccoons' movements slow or fast? What large animal is a near relative of the raccoon?

Color: The raccoon is gray with yellowish shading; the back is dark gray; the face is dirty white with a black patch around each eye; the nose and feet are black; the tail is grayish white ringed with black.

The Raccoon

THE STORY OF THE RACCOON

Questions to be answered and points to be covered in writing the story of

THE FOX

1. Describe the fox's track. How does it differ from the track of a small dog?

2. Where does the fox make its home? Describe the den. Describe the den in which the young foxes live.

3. Describe the red fox, its color and form as completely as you can. What is the expression of its face? What is there peculiar about its tail? What is the use of this great bushy tail in winter?

4. What is the food of the fox? How does it get its food? Is it a day or night hunter? How does the fox benefit the farmer? How does it injure him? How does the fox carry home its heavy game, such as a goose or a hen?

5. Have you ever heard the fox bark? Did it sound like the bark of a dog? How does the fox express anger? Pleasure?

6. When chased by dogs, in what direction does the fox run? Describe all of the tricks which you know by which the fox throws the dog off of the scent.

7. When are the young foxes born? How many in a litter? What color are they? How do they play with each other? How do they learn to hunt?

Color: The fox is brownish red on the back and sides; the tip of the tail is whitish; the legs are black on the outside and whitish on the inside and the feet are black; the throat is white; the ears are tipped with black, also the nose.

The Fox

THE STORY OF THE FOX

Questions to be answered and points to be covered in writing the story of

THE DOG

1. Why are the legs of the dog long and strong in proportion to the body as compared with those of a cat?

2. Compare the feet of the cat with those of the dog and note which has the heavier pads. Why is this of use to each?

3. Which has the stronger and heavier claws, the dog or the cat? Can the dog retract his claws so that they cannot be seen, as does the cat? Of what use is this arrangement to the dog? Are the front feet just like the hind feet? How many toe impressions show in the track of the dog?

4. What is the general characteristic of the body of the dog? Is it soft like that of a cat, or lean and muscular? What is the difference between the hair covering of the dog and cat? How many kinds of gaits has he?

5. Describe the dog's eyes; can he see in the dark? In general, how do the eyes of the dog differ from those of the cat?

6. Study the ear of the dog; is it covered? Is this outer ear movable? How is it used when the dog is listening? Do you think dogs can hear well?

7. Describe the nostrils; are they placed on the foremost point of the face? What is the condition of the skin that surrounds them? How does this condition of the nose aid the dog? Does the dog recognize his friends or become acquainted with strangers by means of his sight or his powers of scent?

8. How does a dog seize and kill his prey? How does he use his feet and claws when fighting? What are his especially strong weapons? Describe a dog's teeth and explain the reason for the bare spaces on the jaw next to the tushes. Does the dog use its tushes when chewing? What teeth does he use when he is gnawing?

9. How by action, voice and especially by the movement of the tail does the dog express the following emotions: Delight, friendliness, affection, attention, anger, fear,shame, excitement? How does he act when chasing his prey? Why do wolves and dogs bark when following the trail?

10. Of what use was the dog to the pioneer? How are dogs used in the Arctic regions? In Holland? In war?

11. How many breeds of dogs do you know? Describe them.

The Dog

THE STORY OF THE DOG

Questions to be answered and points to be covered in writing the story of

THE CAT

1. How much of Pussy's language do you understand? What does she say when you open the door for her? How does she cry when hurt? When frightened? What noise does she make when fighting? When calling other cats? What are her feelings when she purrs? When she spits?

2. How else than by voice does she express affection, pleasure and anger? When she carries her tail straight up in the air, is she in a pleasant mood? When her tail "bristles up?" how does she feel? What is it a sign of, when she lashes her tail back and forth?

3. What do you feed to cats? What do they catch for themselves? What do the cats that are wild live upon? How does the cat help us? How does she injure us?

4. How does a cat catch its prey? Does she track mice by the scent? Does she catch them by running after them as a dog does? Describe how she lies in ambush? How does she hold the mouse as she pounces upon it?

5. Study the cat's paw. Where are the sharp claws? Are they always in sight like a dog's? Does she touch them to the ground when she walks? Describe the cat's foot, including the toe pads. Are there as many toes on the hind feet as on the front feet?

6. Describe a cat's eyes. What is their color? What is the shape of the pupil in the Daylight? In the dark? Describe the inner lid at the corner of the eye.

7. How many teeth has Puss? What is the use of the long tushes? Why is there bare space behind these? Does she use her back teeth for chewing meat?

8. How many whiskers has she? What is their use? Has she a keen sense of smell? Do you think she has a keen sense of hearing? How do the shape and position of the ears help in listening? In what position are the ears when puss is angry?

9. How many colors do you find in our domestic cats? What is the color of wild cats? Why would it not be beneficial to the wild-cat to have as striking colors as our tame cats? Compare the fur of the cat with the hair of a dog. How do they differ? If a cat chased her prey like the dog do you think her fur would be too warm a covering?

10. Describe how the cat washes her face? How does she clean her fur? How does the mother wash her kittens?

11. How does a little kitten look when a day or two old? How long before its eyes open? How does the cat carry her kittens? How does a kitten act when it is being carried? How does the mother cat punish her kittens? How does she teach them to catch mice? How do kittens play?

12. How should cats be trained not to touch birds? When must this training begin?

13. Where in the room does puss best like to lie? How does she sun herself? What herb does she like best?

The Cat

THE STORY OF THE CAT

Questions to be answered and points to be covered in writing the story of

THE HORSE

1. Compare the length of the legs with its height. Has any other domestic animal legs as long in proportion? What habits of the ancestral wild horses led to the development of such long legs?

2. Study the horse's leg and foot. The horse walks on one toe. Which toe is it? What do we call the toe-nail of the horse? Does the hoof grow as our nails do? Make a sketch of the horse's front and hind leg and label those places which correspond to our wrist, elbow, shoulder, hand , heel, knee and hip.

3. Where are the horses' ears placed on the head? How do they move? What do the following different positions of the horse's ear indicate: When lifted and pointing forward? When thrown back?

4. What is the color of the horse's eyes? The shape of the pupil? What advantage does the position of the eyes on the head give to the wild horse? Why do we put blinders on the horse?

5. Look at the mouth and the nose. Are the nostrils large and flaring? Has the horse a keen sense of smell? Are the lips thick or thin? When taking sugar from the hand, does the horse use the teeth or the lips?

6. Describe the horse's teeth. How many front teeth? How many back teeth? Describe the bar where the bit is placed. How can we tell a horse's age by looking at its teeth?

7. What is the nature of the horse's coat in summer? If the horse runs in the pasture all Winter, how does its coat change? What is the use of the horse's mane, forelock and tail? Do you think it is treating the horse well to dock its tail?

8. How does a colt have to place its front legs in order to reach down and eat the grass? Why?

9. When the horse lies down which part goes down first? When getting up which rises first? How does this differ from the method of the cow?

10. In walking, which leg moves first? Second? Third? Fourth? How many gaits has the horse?

11. In fighting, what weapons does the horse use and how?

12. In training a horse, should the voice or the whip be used the most? Why is shying a good quality in wild horses? How should it be dealt with in the domestic horse?

13. What sort of feed is best for the horse? How and when should the horse be watered? Should the water be warmed in cold weather? Why? Should the bit be warmed in winter before putting it in a horse's mouth? Why? Should a tight over-check-rein be used when driving? Why? When the horse has been driven until it is sweating what are the rules for blanketing it when hitched out of doors and which hitched in the barn? What is your opinion of a man who lets his horse stand in waiting in the cold, unblanketed in the village street? Why should dusty hay be dampened before it is fed to a horse? Why should a horse be groomed? Which should receive the most attention in grooming, the legs or the body?

14. How many breeds of horses do you know? What is the use of each?

The Horse

THE STORY OF THE HORSE

Questions to be answered and points to be covered in writing the story of

THE COW

1. What are the characteristics of a fine cow? Describe her horns, ears, eyes, nose and mouth. Do you think she can hear well? What is the attitude of her ears when she is listening? Do you think she has a keen sense of smell? Is her nose moist?

2. The cow walks on two toes. Can you see any other toes in which she does not walk on? What do we call the two hind toes which she does not walk on? Can you point out on the cow's leg those parts which correspond with our elbow, wrist, knee and ankle? Is the cow a good runner? Is she a good jumper? Can she swim?

3. For what use was the cow's tail evidently intended?

4. How does the cow express pleasure? Lonesomeness? Anger? How does the bull express anger? What does the calf express with his voice?

5. How is the leadership of the herd attained? Describe cattle at play.

6. At what time of day do cattle feed in the pasture? When and where do they chew the cud? Do they stand or lie to do this? Describe how a cow lies down and gets up.

7. How do wild cattle defend themselves from wolves? From bears or other solitary animals?

8. For what purposes were cattle first domesticated? For how many purposes do we rear cattle today?

9. Name and give brief descriptions of the different breeds of cattle with which you are familiar. Which if these are beef and which are milch types?

10. What are the distinguishing points of a good milch cow? Of a good beef animal? What does the food do for each of these?

11. How many pounds of milk should a dairy cow produce in a year to be profitable if the product is cheese? If the product is butter? What must be the percent of butter fat in milk to make it legally salable in your state? How many months of the year should a good cow give milk?

12. Why should a cow be milked always by the same person? On which side of the cow does the milker always sit? Why should loud talking and other noise at milking time be avoided? Should a dog be used in driving dairy cows? Why?

13. Why and where is the dehorning of cattle practiced? When and how should a calf be dehorned?

14. For what are oxen used? Wherein are they superior to horses as draft animals? Do you know of any place where oxen are used as riding animals?

15. How many industries are dependent upon cattle?

The Cow

Questions to be answered and points to be covered in writing the story of

THE GOAT

1. Do you think that goats like to climb up to high points? Are they fitted to climb steep, inaccessible places? Can they jump off steep places in safety? How does it happen the goat is sure-footed? How does its legs and feet compare with those of the sheep?

2. What does the goat eat? Where does it find its natural food on mountains? How are the teeth arranged for cutting its food? Does a goat chew its cud like a cow?

3. What is the covering of the goat? Describe a billy-goats beard. Do you suppose this is for ornament? For what is goat's hair used?

4. Do you think the goat has a keen sense of sight, of hearing and of smell? Why? Why did it need to be alert and keen when it lived wild upon the mountains? Do you think a goat is intelligent? Give instances of this.

5. Describe the horns. Do they differ from the horns of the sheep? How does a goat fight? Does he strike head on, like the sheep, or sideways?

6. What noises does the goat make? Do you understand what they mean?

7. Describe some goat which you know. Is the goat's tail short at first or does it have to be cut off like the lamb's tail? Where and how is goat's milk used? What kinds of cheese are made from it? For what is its skin used? Is its flesh ever eaten?

8. Describe a kid and the way it plays.

9. If you have ever had any experiences with a span of goats, describe it.

10. Describe the Angora; for what is it used? What is the difference between the hair of the Angora and Cashmere Goats?

The Goat

THE STORY OF THE GOAT

Questions to be answered and points to be covered in writing the story of

THE SHEEP

1. What is the chief characteristic that separates sheep from other animals? What is the difference between wool and hair?

2. Where do the wild sheep live? What is the climate in those places? Does wool serve them well on this account? What sort of pasturage do sheep find on mountains? Could cows live where sheep thrive? Describe the sheep's teeth and how they are arranged to enable it to crop vegetation closely? Why are sheep not allowed in our forest preserves?

3. What are the chief enemies of the sheep in the wilderness? How do the sheep escape them? Describe the foot and leg of the sheep and explain how they help the animal to escape its enemies. We say of certain men that they 'follow like a flock of sheep.' Why do we make this comparison? What has this habit of following the leader to do with the escape of sheep from wolves and bears?

4. How do sheep fight? Do both rams and ewes have horns? Do they both fight? How does the sheep show anger? Give your experience with a cross cosset lamb if you have any..

5. Do you think that sheep can see and hear well? What is the position of the sheep's ears when it is peaceful? When there is danger? How do the sheeps' eyes differ from those of the cow?

6. Does the sheep chew its cud like the cow? Describe the action as performed by the sheep. How is this habit of cud chewing of use to the wild sheep?

7. Describe a young lamb. Why has it such long legs? How does it use its tail to express joy? What happens to this tail later? What games have you seen lambs play?

8. How much of sheep language do you understand? What is the use to the wild flock of the constant bleating?

9. For what purpose do we keep sheep? How many breeds of sheep do you know? What are the chief differences between the English breeds and the Merinos? Where and for what purpose is the milk of sheep used?

10. Have you ever seen a collie looking after a flock of sheep? If so, describe its actions. Did you ever know of dogs killing sheep? At what time of day or night was this done? Did you ever know of one dog attacking a flock of sheep alone? What is there in the dogs ancestry which makes two or three dogs, when hunting, attack sheep?

The Sheep

THE STORY OF THE GOAT

Questions to be answered and points to be covered in writing the story of

THE PIG

1. How does the pig's nose differ from that of other animals? What is it used for besides smelling? Do you think that the pig's sense of smell is very keen? Why do pigs root?

2. Describe the pig's teeth. For what are they fitted? What are the tusks for? Which way do the upper tusks turn? How do wild hogs use their tusks?

3. Do you think that a pig's eyes look intelligent? What color are they? Do you think the pig can see well?

4. Is the pig's head straight in front or is it dished? Is this dished appearance ever found in wild hogs? Do the ears stand out straight or are they lopped? What advantage is the wedge-shaped head to the wild hog?

5. How is the pig covered? Do you think the hair is thick enough to keep off flies? Why does the pig wallow in the mud? Is it because the animal is dirty by nature or because it is trying to keep clean? Do the hog's bristles stand up if it is angry?

6. If the pig could have its natural food what would it be and where would it be found? Why and on what should pigs be pastured? What do pigs find in the forest to eat? What kind of bacon is considered the best?

7. On how many toes does the pig walk? Are there other toes on which it does not walk? If wading in the mud, are the two hind toes of use? Do wild pigs run rapidly? Do tame pigs run rapidly if they are not too fat? Do you think the pig can swim? Do you think that the pig's tail is of any use or merely an ornament?

8. What cries and noises do the pigs make which we can understand?

9. How do hogs fight each other? When the boars fight, how do they attack or ward off the enemy? Where do we get the expression going "side wise like a hog to war?"

10. How many breeds of pig do you know? Describe them.

11. What instances have you heard that show the hog's intelligence?

The Pig

THE STORY OF THE PIG

Questions to be answered and points to be covered in writing the story of

THE PRAIRIE DOG

1. Where in the United States does the prairie dog live?

2. Describe the burrow in which the prairie dog lives. Are there many of these burrows near together, so that they form a village?

3. What are the enemies of the prairie dog? How does it keep watch for them? Describe the tower on which it sits while on guard.

4. How does it escape its enemies? How do the prairie dogs of a village get rid of a snake?

5. On what do the prairie dogs feed? On the great dry plans east of the Rocky Mountains, the vegetation on which they feed is scanty; what do they do when all the vegetation is eaten up around one of their villages? How are the prairie dogs affecting the farmer on the great plains.

6. Describe how a prairie dog holds it's food while eating.; does it store food, if so where?

7. What noises does it make and what do they mean?

8. Tell how the burrowing owls live with the prairie dogs.

Color: The prairie dog is brownish yellow above and dirty white below; the tail is tipped with black.

The Prairie Dog

THE STORY OF THE PRAIRIE DOG

Questions to be answered and points to be covered in writing the story of

THE TOAD

1. Describe the general color of the toad above and below. How does the toad's back look? Of what use are the warts on its back?

2. Where is the toad usually found? Does it feel warm or cold to the hand? Is it slimy or dry? The toad is a cold-blooded animal, what does this mean?

3. Describe the eyes and explain how their situation is of special advantage to the toad. Do you think it can see in front and behind and above all at the same time? Does the bulge of the eyes help in this? How does the toad wink?

4. Find and describe the nostrils.. Find and describe the ear. Note the swelling above and just back of the ear.

5. What is the shape of the toad's mouth? Has it any teeth? Is the toads tongue attached to the front or the back part of the mouth? How is it used to catch insects?

6. Describe the 'arms and hands.' How many 'fingers' on the 'hand?' Which way do the fingers point when the toad is sitting down?

7. Describe the legs and feet. How many toes are there? What is the relative length of the toes and how are they connected? What is the web between the toes for? Why are the hind legs so much larger than the front legs?

8. Where does the toad live? When it is disturbed, how does it act? How far can it jump? If very frightened does it flatten out and lie still? Why is this?

9. At what time does the toad come out to hunt insects? How does it catch the insect? Does it swallow an earthworm head or tail first? When swallowing a large insect, how does it use its hands? How does it act when swallowing a large mouthful?

10. How does the toad drink? Where does it remain during the day? Describe how it burrows into the earth.

11. What happens to the toad in winter? What does it do in the spring? Is it a good swimmer?

12. How does the toad look when croaking? What sort of noise does it make? What are the toads enemies?

13. 1How is the toad of great use to the farmer and gardener?

14. Where are the toads' eggs found and on what date? Were they attached to anything in the water or were they floating free? Are the eggs in long strings? Do you find any eggs laid jelly-like masses? If so, what are they?

15. Describe a tadpole - how and where it lives and how it changes into a toad.

Color: The toad is yellowish brown above with warts darker and whiteish underneath; its eyes are golden.

The Toad

THE STORY OF THE TOAD

Questions to be answered and points to be covered in writing the story of

THE MOUSE

1. Why is the color of the mouse of special benefit to it? Do you think it protects it from the sight of its enemies? Can you see a mouse easily as it runs across the room?

2. How long is a mouse's tail as compared with its body? What is the covering of the tail? Of what use to the mouse is this long rigid tail? Watch the mouse carefully and discover, if you can, the use of the tail in climbing.

3. Is the mouse a good jumper? Are the hind legs long and strong when compared with the front legs? How high do you think a mouse can jump? Do you think it uses its tail as an aid when jumping? How much of the legs are covered with hair? Compare the front and hind feet. What sort of claws have they? How does the mouse use its feet when climbing? How can it climb up the side of a wall?

4. Describe the eyes. Do you think the mouse can see very well? Does it wink? What is the shape of the ears? Do you think it can hear well? Can it move its ears forward or backward?

5. What is the shape of the snout? Of what advantage is this? Note the whiskers. What is their use? Describe the mouth. Do you know how the teeth are arranged? For what other use other than to bite food does the mouse use its teeth? What other animals have their teeth arranged like those of the mouse? What food does the mouse live upon?

6. How does the mouse act when it is reaching up to examine something? How does it hold its front feet? Describe how the mouse washes its face. It's back. It's feet.

7. Where does the mouse build its nest? Of what material? How do the baby mice look? Can they see when they are first born?

8. House mice are great travelers. Can you tell how they get from place to place?

9. How many kinds of mice do you know? Does the house mouse ever live in the field? What do you know of the habits of the white-footed mouse? Of the meadow mice? Of the jumping mice?

Color: The house mouse is yellowish gray above and paler gray below with the feet and nose pinkish.

The Mouse

THE STORY OF THE MOUSE

Questions to be answered and points to be covered in writing the story of

THE FERRET

1. How large is the ferret? What does it feed upon? How does it follow and kill its prey? How does the form of the ferret assist it while hunting? Why is it called blood-thirsty? Does it follow its prey by sight or by smell?

2. What is the color of the ferret's fur?

3. Where does the ferret make its den?

4. How does the ferret resemble the weasel in appearance and methods of hunting?

5. The skunk, the marten, the wolverine, the mink, the fisher, and the otter all belong to the same family as the ferret. Tell what you know of these, noting especially how many of them get their food in the water, and how many on land?

Color: In summer, the ferret is dark reddish brown above with underpart white; the tail is black at the top and for one third of its length.

The Ferret

THE STORY OF THE FERRET

Questions to be answered and points to be covered in writing the story of

THE SNAKE

1. What are the colors and markings of your snake? Do the stripes extend along the head as well as the body? How long is it?

2. Describe its eyes, its ears, its nostrils and its mouth.

3. If you disturb it, how does it act? Why does it thrust its tongue out? What shape is its tongue?

4. In what position is the snake when it rests? Can you see how it moves? Look upon the lower side. Can you see the little plates extending crosswise? Do you think it moves by moving these plates? Let it crawl across your hand, and see if you can tell how it moves.

5. What does the snake eat? Did you ever see one swallow a toad or a frog? Did it take its head first or tail first? How does it catch its prey?

6. Where does the snake spend its winter? How early does it appear in the spring?

7. At what time of year do you see the young snakes? Does the mother snake defend her young?

8. What enemies has the snake?

Color: The snake should be colored according to the specimen under observation. The garter snake is dark brown or greenish black above with a yellow whiteish stripe down the center of the back and a stripe not so bright along each side; the lower side is yellowish or greenish white.

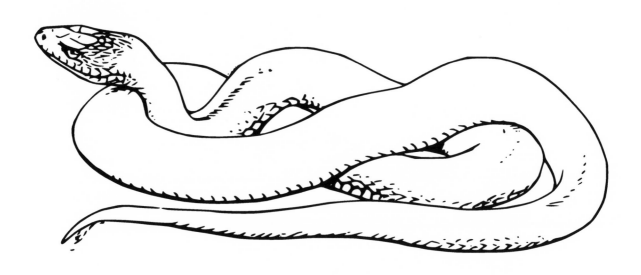

The Snake

THE STORY OF THE SNAKE

Questions to be answered and points to be covered in writing the story of

THE GUINEA PIG

1. What is the general shape of the guinea pig's body? It's head? Describe the ears; are they movable? Describe the eyes.

2. Describe the mouth; note the shape of the teeth and how they are arranged. Are there any whiskers about the mouth? Are these sensitive when you touch them?

3. Describe the feet; Is there the same number of toes on the front as on the hind feet? Are the claws strong?

4. Place a guinea pig on some soil or gravel and note how it digs; which feet does it use in digging? Since it lives in a borrow naturally, of what advantage to it is it's very short tail? Does it run rapidly? Does it jump when running?

5. When it eats, which teeth does it use to bite off food and which does it use when chewing? Describe how it eats a blade of grass.

6. How does a guinea pig wash its face? How does it clean its body? What noises does it make, and what do these noises mean?

7. Describe the hair of the guinea pig.

8. How would you take care of guinea pigs to keep them well and comfortable? What kind of food would you give them, and what kind of a house to live in?

The Guinea Pig

THE STORY OF THE SNAKE

Questions to be answered and points to be covered in writing the story of

THE PORCUPINE

1. What is the most noticeable thing about the porcupine? What are his natural enemies? How does the porcupine quill punish any enemy that attacks him? How does the porcupine act when attacked?

2. Does the protection through his coat of spears render the porcupine free from fear? What effect has this safety from attack had upon the porcupines' wits? People have said that the porcupines could throw his quills. How do we know that this cannot be true? When very young, does the porcupine have quills?

3. On what does this animal live? And how does it get its food? How and why does it injure the property of campers and maple maple sugar makers?

4. Where does it make its home?

Color: The hair of the porcupine is dark brown, almost black; the quills have yellowish tips so that the animal seems to be dark brown washed with yellowish.

The Porcupine

THE STORY OF THE PORCUPINE

Questions to be answered and points to be covered in writing the story of

THE NEWT

1. Look at the newt closely. Is it all the same color? How many spots upon its back and what colors are they? Are there the same number of spots on both sides? Are there any spots or dots besides the larger ones?

2. Is the head the widest part of the body? Describe the eyes, the shape and color of the pupil and of the iris. How does the newt wink? Do you think it can see well? Can you see the nostrils? How does the throat move and why?

3. Are both pairs of legs the same size? How many toes on the front feet? How many toes on the hind feed? Does the newt toe-in with its front feet like a toad?

4. Does it move more than one foot at a time when walking? Does it use the feet on the same side in two consecutive steps? After putting forward the right front foot, what foot follows next? Can it move backward?

5. Is the tail as long as the head and body together? Is the tail round or flat at the sides? How is it used to help the newt when traveling? Does the tail drag or is it lifted, or does it push by squirming?

6. How does the newt act when startled? Does it examine its surroundings? Do you think it can see and is afraid of you?

7. Why do we find these creatures only during wet weather? Why do people think they rain down?

8. What does the newt eat? How does it catch its prey? Does it shed its skin? How many kinds of newts have you seen?

9. From what kind of egg does the eft hatch? When is this egg laid? How does it look? On what is it fastened?

10. How many times during its life does the orange newt change color? What part of its life is spent upon land? What changes take place in its form when it leaves the water for life upon land, and what changes take place in its structure when it returns to the water?

Color: The salamander should be colored according to the species under observation; it may be black with yellow spots or all blue black above and reddish below or it maybe orange red above, lighter orange below with five vermilion spots bordered with black dots on each side and the sides peppered with tiny black dots.

The Newt

THE STORY OF THE NEWT

.

Made in the USA
Monee, IL
05 September 2021